World Book's Learning Ladders

Community Helpers

WORLD BOOK

a Scott Fetzer company
Chicago
www.worldbookonline.com

WORLD
BOOK

233 N. Michigan Avenue
Chicago, IL 60601
U.S.A.

For information about other World Book publications, visit our Web site at
http://www.worldbookonline.com or call **1-800-WORLDBK (967-5325)**.

For information about sales to schools and libraries, call **1-800-975-3250 (United States)**;
1-800-837-5365 (Canada).

Library of Congress Cataloging-in-Publication Data

Community helpers.
     p. cm. -- (World Book's learning ladders)
   Includes index.
   Summary: "Introduction to people who work in a
community using simple text, illustrations, and photos.
Features include puzzles and games, fun facts, a
resource list, and an index"--Provided by publisher.
   ISBN 978-0-7166-7737-6
   1. Community life--Juvenile literature. 2. Communities--
Juvenile literature. 3. Human services--Juvenile
literature. I. World Book, Inc.
HM761.C63 2011
307--dc22
                                        2010022379

World Book's Learning Ladders
Set 2 ISBN: 978-0-7166-7746-8

Printed in China
by Shenzhen Wing King Tong Paper Products Co., Ltd.
Shenzhen, Guangdong
2nd printing May 2012

Editorial
  Editor in Chief: Paul A. Kobasa
  Associate Manager, Supplementary Publications:
    Cassie Mayer
  Writer: Shawn Brennan
  Researcher: Cheryl Graham
  Manager, Contracts & Compliance
  (Rights & Permissions): Loranne K. Shields
Manufacturing/Pre-Press/Graphics and Design
  Director: Carma Fazio
  Manufacturing Manager: Steven K. Hueppchen
  Senior Production Manager: Janice Rossing
  Production/Technology Manager: Anne Fritzinger
  Proofreader: Emilie Schrage
  Senior Manager, Graphics and Design: Tom Evans
  Coordinator, Design Development and Production:
    Brenda B. Tropinski

  Photographs Editor: Kathy Creech

Photographic credits: Cover: © Blend Images/SuperStock; WORLD BOOK illustration by Q2A Media;
Shutterstock; p2, p5, p9, p26, p27, p28, p30: Shutterstock; p5, p6, p8, p18: Alamy Images;
p10, p11, p14, p16: AP Images; p19, p21, p22: Getty Images

Illustrators: WORLD BOOK illustration by Q2A Media

What's inside?

This book tells you about some of the people in your community who help you and your family. We see some of these people every day. But there are also people who help us whom we do not see very often.

Teacher

Teachers play an important role in a community. A community is a group of people who live in the same area. Your neighborhood is a community. So is your city or town. Teachers are people in a community who help us learn. Some teachers work with children. Others help adults learn.

A **map** helps us find different places around the world.

A **school librarian** helps teach the lesson.

A **student** raises her hand to ask a question.

Students use a **pencil and paper** to take notes.

WORLD MAP

A teacher writes a lesson on a **whiteboard**.

MOUNTA NGES THE WORLD

Librarians work in school or public libraries. They help people find and use information.

5

Bus driver

Bus drivers help people in a community get from place to place. Some bus drivers help us get to school. Others drive on certain routes (paths) around town. Bus drivers must have a special license to drive a bus.

A bus driver picks up people at a **bus stop**.

Many other workers help people get from place to place. Some workers drive trains that take people into cities.

BUS STOP

Buses have numbers that show their **route**.

The screen on the front of the bus shows the bus's **destination**.

56 SHOPPING DISTRICT

Bus drivers help people with **directions**.

Passengers pay to get on the bus. They can use money or a **fare card**.

It's a fact!

The word *bus* comes from a longer word, *omnibus* (AHM *nih buhs*). This Latin word means "for everyone."

7

Mail carrier

Mail carriers help people in a community send and receive letters and packages. Many workers handle mail as it travels from place to place. Mail carriers collect mailed letters from a mailbox. They also deliver mail to homes and businesses.

Each **letter** must have enough **stamps** to pay for postage.

Postal workers sort and process mail at a post office.

Some mail carriers use a **cart** to carry mail.

Some mail carriers deliver the mail by bicycle.

People place letters in a **mailbox**. A mail carrier collects these letters.

A mail carrier wears a special **uniform**.

It's a fact!

Pigeons, camels, horses, reindeer, dogs, and cats have at times been used to deliver mail!

Garbage collector

A **garbage truck** takes trash to a dump or recycling center.

Garbage collectors help keep the community clean. They pick up garbage from homes and businesses. Other workers also help keep the community clean. They may sweep or hose down streets.

Garbage collectors follow certain routes (paths). They collect garbage from houses on their route.

Garbage collectors pick up **garbage cans** along each route on a certain day of the week.

Workers at recycling centers break down old paper, plastic, metal, and glass items. These materials are then used to make new items.

Some workers in a community test water in lakes and rivers to make sure it is clean.

County
Sanitation

It's a fact!

In 1981, garbage piled high in Vancouver, Canada. There was no garbage collection in the city for more than three months!

The garbage collector empties the garbage into the truck's **hopper.**

On the way to school

You see community helpers every day! What kinds of helpers do you see in this picture?

BUS STOP

47 SHOPPING DISTRICT

12

Words you know

Here are some words that you learned earlier. Say them out loud, then try to find the things in the picture.

library   garbage truck

uniform   letter

bus stop   passenger

LIBRARY

ONE WAY

SCHOOL

Where has the bus driver stopped the bus?

13

Where is the garbage collector placing the trash?

Lawmaker

A lawmaker is a person who makes laws. Laws are rules that people must follow. Lawmakers represent the people of a community. They work to protect the people. People become lawmakers by winning elections. People in the community vote to elect (choose) their lawmakers.

A **campaign sign** shows the name of a person running for office.

Judges are people who work in courts of law. People go to court to settle disputes or when they are accused of breaking the law.

A **capitol building** is where lawmakers meet to make and vote on laws.

A **lawmaker** makes a speech. She tells how she will work to make the community better for everyone.

News reporters report on what the lawmaker says.

It's a fact!

The Althing *(AHL thihng)* of Iceland is the world's oldest lawmaking group. It was formed more than 1,000 years ago!

Police officer

Police officers help to keep a community safe. They make sure people follow the law. They arrest people who break the law. Police officers also help protect people from danger. The big picture shows police officers who are helping people after a car accident.

Police officers wear **uniforms and badges** to identify themselves.

A police officer writes a **report** about an accident.

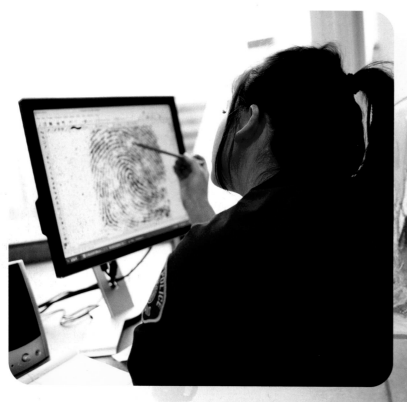

Police officers use computers that record and match people's fingerprints. This helps them to catch criminals.

Police officers talk to each other on **two-way radios**.

It's a fact!

The most common dog breed that assists police officers is the German shepherd.

A police officer drives a **squad car**.

A squad car's **flashing lights** and loud siren let people know that police need to get to a place quickly.

Firefighter

Firefighters put out fires in a community. They rescue people from fires. They also try to save buildings, forests, and other things that catch on fire. Firefighters often help police and medical workers in emergencies. They also teach people how to prevent fires.

Fireproof clothes help to keep firefighters safe from heat and flames.

Fire stations have kitchens and a place for firefighters to sleep.

Firefighters use a **hose** to spray water on the fire.

Firefighters slide down a **pole** from upstairs to get to the truck quickly.

Fire trucks carry special equipment for fighting fires.

Firefighters use airplanes to help fight forest fires. The airplane sprays a chemical that helps put out the fire.

It's a fact!

Before modern firefighting equipment was developed, people fought fires by forming a line and passing buckets of water from person to person.

19

Medical worker

Doctors, nurses, and other medical workers take care of sick or injured people. Paramedics are medical workers who ride in ambulances. They take care of people who have been in an accident or who suddenly become ill. The paramedics shown here are bringing a patient to a hospital.

Doctors take over the care of the patient at the hospital.

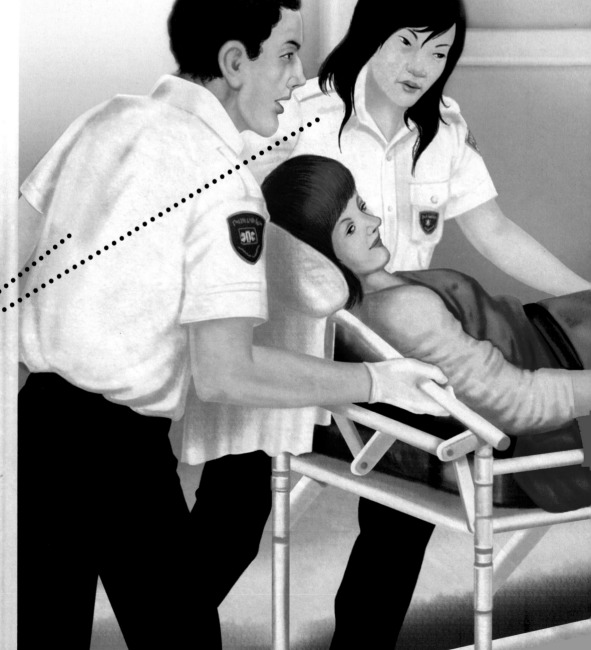

Paramedics drive an ambulance. The ambulance carries injured people to the hospital.

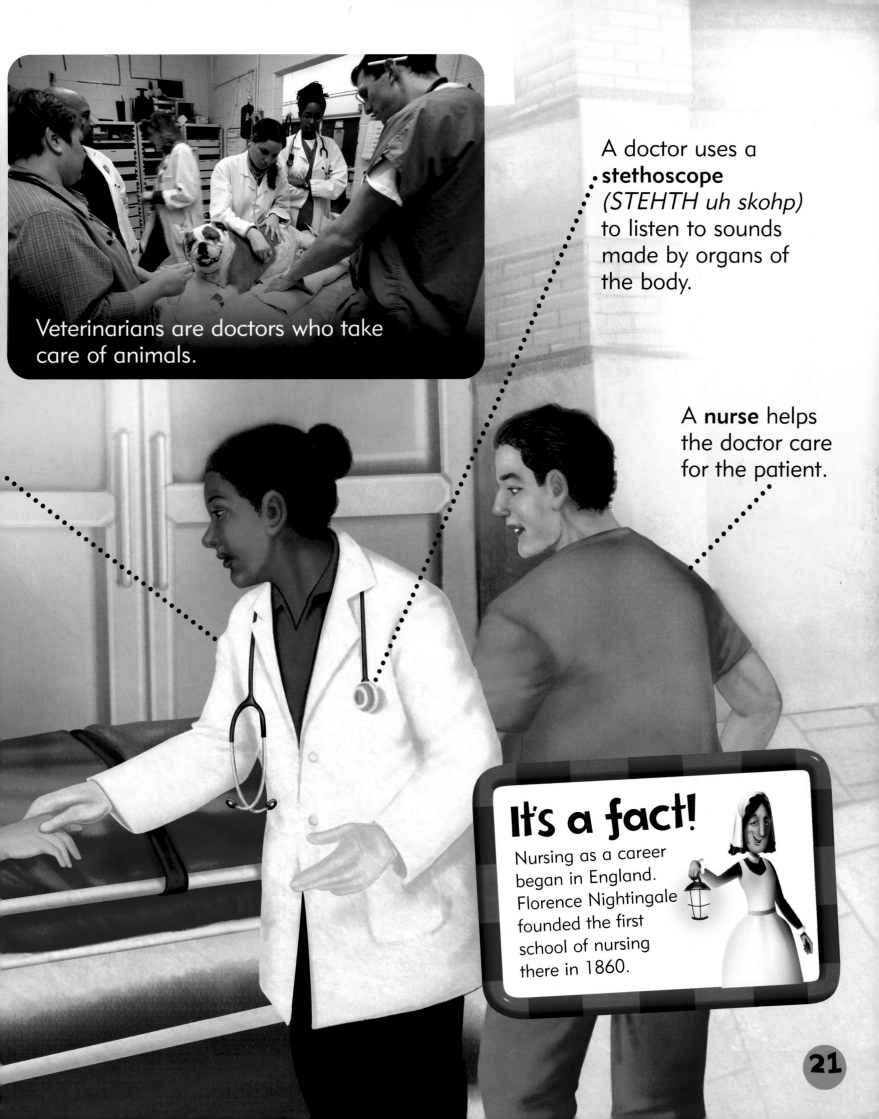

Veterinarians are doctors who take care of animals.

A doctor uses a **stethoscope** *(STEHTH uh skohp)* to listen to sounds made by organs of the body.

A **nurse** helps the doctor care for the patient.

It's a fact!

Nursing as a career began in England. Florence Nightingale founded the first school of nursing there in 1860.

Utility worker

Utility workers perform many important services. Some help to bring clean water to our homes and remove wastewater. Others provide natural gas to heat homes and power stoves. Still others provide telephone service.

Utility workers must be careful when working around electric power lines.

A **manhole** allows utility workers to get to underground .... wires.

22

Power lines carry electricity across cities and towns.

Utility workers use special **equipment** to reach wires high in the sky.

Utility workers use special **tools** to work on power lines.

23

Around town

Look at all the busy people working very hard in your community! They help to make your neighborhood safe and better for everyone to live in.

Words you know

Here are some words that you learned earlier. Say them out loud, then try to find the things in the picture.

fire hydrant   capitol

ambulance   siren

hose   police officer

24

Which vehicles have sirens?

25

Did you know?

Until the 1800's, most people never attended school. By the mid-1800's, the United States, Canada, and many European countries had established public school systems.

Before the invention of writing, people could only pass along knowledge through word of mouth.

The badge of a police officer is a symbol of law and authority.

One of the first firefighting organizations was established in ancient Rome.

About 58 million men and women throughout the world are teachers.

Post offices in some countries handle people's money as well as their mail.

Mr. Smith
414 State Street
Chicago, Il 60601

Puzzles

Double trouble!

These two pictures are not exactly the same. Can you find the five things that are different in picture b?

a

b

Answers on page 32.

28

Going to work...

Can you figure out where each community helper is headed for work? Follow the lines to find out!

Match up!

Match each word on the left with its picture on the right.

a

1. garbage collector

b

2. teacher

c

3. firefighter

d

4. police officer

e

5. utility worker

f

6. bus driver

Answers on page 32.

True or false

Can you figure out which of these statements are true? Turn to the page numbers given to help you find the answers.

Lawmakers are elected to office.
Go to page 14.

3

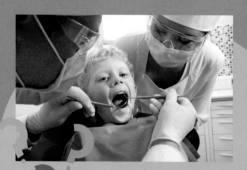

Veterinarians help care for people's teeth.
Go to page 21.

1

4

People place stamps on letters to pay for postage.
Go to page 8.

Bus drivers must have a special license to drive a bus.
Go to page 6.

2

Police officers help to catch criminals.
Go to page 16.

5

Answers on page 32.

Find out more

Books

Crafts for Kids Who Are Learning About Community Workers by Kathy Ross (Millbrook Press, 2006)
The projects in this book are all about the things that community workers do to help you.

Neighborhood Helpers by Jennifer Blizin Gillis (Rourke Publishing, 2007)
Learn about people who work in many communities.

Neighborhood Helpers by Cecilia Minden and others (Child's World, 2006). Twelve volumes: *Auto Mechanics, Coaches, Dentists, Electricians, Firefighters, Letter Carriers, Nurses, Pilots, Restaurant Owners, Teachers, Television Reporters, Veterinarians.*
Read books in this series to learn more about the many different jobs people have in every community.

People in the Community by Diyan Leake (Heinemann-Raintree, 2009). Six volumes: *Dentists, Doctors, Firefighters, Police Officers, Teachers, Vets.*
Learn about people in your community and the work that they do.

Web sites

Be a Volunteer
http://kidshealth.org/kid/feeling/thought/volunteering.html
Offers suggestions on how kids and families can help community workers by volunteering to be a helper themselves.

Ben's Guide to U.S. Government for Kids
http://bensguide.gpo.gov/k-2/neighborhood/
Describes work at a fire station, hospital, library, police station, post office, and school, with links to the related government agency that offers more information.

Community Helpers Theme
http://www.first-school.ws/theme/commhelpers.htm
Fifteen community workers are listed, with links to activities and crafts related to their jobs.

Answers

Puzzles
from pages 28 and 29

Double trouble!
In picture b, the green building in the background is missing, the word "mail" is missing from the mailbox, the bow on the girl's left pigtail is missing, the flowers are orange, and the clouds are missing.

Match up!
1. c
2. f
3. d
4. e
5. a
6. b

True or false
from page 30

1. false
2. true
3. true
4. true
5. true

Index